American Holidays
LABOR DAY
Connor Dayton

PowerKiDS press™

New York

Published in 2012 by The Rosen Publishing Group, Inc.
29 East 21st Street, New York, NY 10010

First Edition

Editor: Jennifer Way
Book Design: Julio Gil

Photo Credits: Cover © www.iStockphoto.com/Sean Locke; pp. 5, 15, 20–21, 23, 24 (top left, top right) Shutterstock.com; p. 7 Bill Pugliano/Getty Images; p. 9 Topical Press Agency/Getty Images; p. 11 Stock Montage/Getty Images; p. 13 Thinkstock Images/Comstock/Thinkstock; pp. 17, 24 (bottom) Susan Watts/NY Daily News Archive via Getty Images; p. 19 Jamie Sabau/Getty Images.

Library of Congress Cataloging-in-Publication Data

Dayton, Connor.
 Labor day / by Connor Dayton. — 1st ed.
     p. cm. — (American holidays)
 Includes index.
 ISBN 978-1-4488-6147-7 (library binding) — ISBN 978-1-4488-6252-8 (pbk.) —
ISBN 978-1-4488-6253-5 (6-pack)
 1. Labor day—United States—Juvenile literature. I. Title.
 HD7791.D39 2012
 394.264—dc23
                                    2011027186

Manufactured in the United States of America

CPSIA Compliance Information: Batch #WW12PK: For Further Information contact Rosen Publishing, New York, New York at 1-800-237-9932

Contents

Labor Day is the first Monday in September.

Labor Day honors the fight for workers' rights.

Workers spoke out for safety and shorter workdays.

8

President Grover Cleveland made Labor Day a holiday in 1894.

Labor Day honors American workers. Most people have the day off.

People have **cookouts** on Labor Day.

Many cities have **parades**. The first Labor Day parade was in New York City.

District Council No. 9
International Union of Painters & Alli...

17

Labor Day is also the start of football season.

People go to the **beach** on Labor Day. Long Beach in Washington is America's longest beach.

What do you do on Labor Day?

Words to Know

beach

cookout

parade

Index

Web Sites

Due to the changing nature of Internet links, PowerKids Press has developed an online list of Web sites related to the subject of this book. This site is updated regularly. Please use this link to access the list: www.powerkidslinks.com/amh/labor/

24